Advance Praise for

# Lean Against This Late Hour

"Reading Abdolmalekian's poems is like happening upon a system of non-Euclidean geometry: shapes so clearly rendered, so seemingly inevitable, that you're stunned you had never encountered them before. But then you realize that these elegantly simple lines, in fact, interpenetrate multiple dimensions. The natural and the political, phenomenology and sexuality, reason and imagination fuse into new and compelling hybrids. Only in language can these concepts occupy the same space, and I'm profoundly grateful that English-language readers have, at long last, been offered access to this work."

—Monica Youn, author of *Blackacre*

"Garous Abdolmalekian's *Lean Against This Late Hour* delves deep into the solitary melancholy heart of a poet gripped by the buried secrets of Iran's historical trauma. With aching intimacy, Abdolmalekian takes dreamlike inventory of the deaths that hang over him. He writes with orphic clarity the silence that the state has imposed upon him, and takes a shred of darkness that enshrouds his country and whets it to a blade that sings. This is a powerful, searching, and timeless collection of poems."

—Cathy Park Hong, author of
*Engine Empire* and *Minor Feelings*

lean against this late hour

# lean against
# this late hour

## GAROUS
## ABDOLMALEKIAN

Translated from the Persian
by Ahmad Nadalizadeh and Idra Novey

PENGUIN POETS

PENGUIN BOOKS
An imprint of Penguin Random House LLC
penguinrandomhouse.com

LIBRARY OF CONGRESS CATALOGING-IN-PUBLICATION DATA
Names: 'Abd al-Malikiyān, Garūs, 1980– author. |
Nadalizadeh, Ahmad, translator. | Novey, Idra, translator. |
'Abd al-Malikiyān, Garūs, 1980– Poems. Selections. English. |
'Abd al-Malikiyān, Garūs, 1980– Poems. Selections.
Title: Lean against this late hour / Garous Abdolmalekian ;
translated from the Persian by Ahmad Nadalizadeh and Idra Novey.
Description: New York : Penguin Books, 2020. | Series: Penguin poets
Identifiers: LCCN 2019036463 (print) | LCCN 2019036464 (ebook) |
ISBN 9780143134930 (paperback) | ISBN 9780525506607 (ebook)
Classification: LCC PK6562.1.B23 A2 2020 (print) | LCC PK6562.1.B23 (ebook) |
DDC 891/.5514—dc23
LC record available at https://lccn.loc.gov/2019036463
LC ebook record available at https://lccn.loc.gov/2019036464

Printed in the United States of America
1   3   5   7   9   10   8   6   4   2

Book design by Daniel Lagin

# Contents

# Introduction

Born eighteen days after the outbreak of the Iran-Iraq War in 1980, Garous Abdolmalekian is one of the most prominent figures in Iran's contemporary literary landscape. He has had an enormous influence on the new generation of Iranian poets addressing the dramatic social changes under way in the country. The author of six award-winning books and an editor at a leading publishing house in Tehran, Abdolmalekian has become a pivotal voice among poets in Iran determined to convey the inner life of their country and the stifled songs emerging from the silence in which they came of age.

While the force in many of Abdolmalekian's poems is political, his approach to them is fabulist. In "Border," he brings the blasts of a battle into the sheets of a couple's bed. In "Bits of Darkness," a man shot the day before continues hoping to be released into another sunrise, though he's been dead for twenty-four hours. In Abdolmalekian's poems, even the dead go on hoping for intimations of a kinder world. Yet his images never retreat into any kind of easy, blind escape from reality. Instead, they chart the difficulty of not just accepting but prevailing over unspeakable violence and loss. His sensorial images flip the private into the political with a deceptively subversive subtlety and also with startling intimacy. An injured veteran begs his mother to change his diapers. An unspoken death manifests in the dust circulating in a room, aching to be kissed. The political impetus in an Abdolmalekian poem is never evoked directly. Rather, it is left to flow quietly, powerfully, beneath the poem, the unseen groundwater of each speaker's life.

Abdolmalekian's style has been described as cinematic, inspired by his love of Iranian film directors such as Abbas Kiarostami who themselves look to contemporary Persian poetry for their aesthetic. Abdolmalekian's work turns this cinema back into poetry, inviting the reader into poems as unpredictable in their sequencing as the stills of a film, with the reader bearing witness to the poems' unfolding in both time and space. The poems are thus not only a description of an event, but an invitation for the reader to experience the narrator's bewilderment alongside all the contradictory reactions that bewilderment demands, as in "Long Poem of Loneliness," in which time dissembles line by line:

> He stands up
> to go sit by the window
> realizes he has been sitting
> by the window for hours.

The reader comes to experience the emerging impossibility of enduring this afternoon in tandem with the lonely character of the poem. In the blink of an eye the world becomes increasingly unworlded, devoid of even the reliable relief of a sunset.

Abdolmalekian has received numerous prizes for his groundbreaking poems in Iran, and his work has been translated into nine languages, with this collection marking the first book-length translation of his work into English. We hope this introduction to one of Iran's most celebrated new poets will invite English-language readers to join the larger global conversation about his astonishing work. Translating a poet who responds to contemporary events with such a latent metaphorical language can be tricky. How many of his subtle allusions will be apparent to English-language readers, and how many will be lost—this was a constant concern during the translation process. We have done our best to re-create the allusions with as much subtlety as they contain in Persian, with all their fascinating multiplicity of potential interpretations and meanings. Abdolmalekian's poetry evokes the nuances of the country around him with an urgency evident in the new generation of poets in the United States as well. Young urban poets all over the world are deeply questioning the history and the future of their countries. Abdolmalekian's haunting, fable-like poems feel as timeless as they are frank and contemporary. His work breathes new life into the ancient art of poetry and how the form may forecast the interior experience of the century ahead.

—Ahmad Nadalizadeh and Idra Novey

lean against this late hour

# مرز

دراز کشیده‌ام
زنم شعری از جنگ می‌خوانَد،
همین مانده بود
تانک‌ها به تختخوابم بیایند

گلوله‌ها
خواب‌هایم را
سوراخ سوراخ کرده‌اند
بر یکی از آنها چشم می‌گذاری:
خیابانی می‌بینی
که برف پوستش را سفید کرده است . . .
کاش برف نمی‌آمد
که مرزِ ملافه و خیابان پیدا بود

حالا تانک‌ها
از خاکریز ملافه‌های تخت گذشته‌اند و
کم‌کم به خوابم وارد می‌شوند:
من بچه بودم
مادرم ظرف می‌شست
و پدر با سبیل سیاهش به خانه برمی‌گشت،
بمب‌ها که می‌باریدند
هرسه بچه بودیم . . .
تصویرهای بعدی این خواب
خفه‌ات می‌کند!
چشم‌هایت را ببند
لب بر این دریچه‌ی کوچک بگذار
و تنها نفس بکش
نفس بکش
نفس بکش!
نفس بکش!
نفس بکش لعنتی!
نفس بکش!
نفس!

## Border

I am in repose
as my wife reads a poem about war

The last thing I need
is for the tanks to advance into my bed

Bullets have made numerous holes
in my dreams

You put your eye up to one of them:
you see a street
its skin whitened with snow
if only it did not snow
if the borders between the streets and the bedcovers were clear

Now the tanks have crossed the trenches into our bedsheets
and one by one they enter my dream:
I was a kid
my mother washed the dishes
and my father returned home with his black mustache
When the bombs poured forth
all three of us were children . . .
The following pictures of this dream will tighten your chest
Shut your eyes
Put your lips on this little vent
and just breathe
Just breathe
Breathe!
Breathe!
Damn it!
Just breathe!
Breathe!

دکتر سرش را تکان می‌دهد
پرستار سرش را تکان می‌دهد
دکتر عرقش را پاک می‌کند
و رشته کوه‌های سبز
برصفحه‌ی مانیتور
کویر می‌شوند

The doctor shakes his head
The nurse shakes her head
The doctor wipes the sweat from his brow
And the green mountain chain
on the screen
turns to desert.

## طرح

پیراهنت در باد تکان می‌خورد
این
تنها پرچمی است که دوستش دارم

## Pattern

Your dress waving in the wind.
This
is the only flag I love.

## باید کنار بیایم

وزنِ یک خبر در گوشیِ تلفن
که سنگینش می‌کند
می‌اندازد آن را از دست‌های من

وزنِ بی‌دلیلِ بعضی چیزها
تکه‌ای فلز در خرابه‌ای متروک

حالت خمیده‌ی پدر
که بعدِ سال‌ها، هنوز
مُرده‌ی برادرم را از دوش
بر زمین نگذاشته است
باید کنار بیایم
باید بیایم کنار
مگر چند دقیقه‌ی دیگر می‌شود
به راه رفتن وسطِ این اتوبان ادامه داد؟

بوق‌ها تنهاترم می‌کنند
و تنهاترم می‌کنند
و تنهاترم می‌کنند
چرا کسی را که تنها می‌ماند، خاک می‌کنید؟

هیچ مرگی طبیعی نیست
این شعر به بیمارستان نمی‌رسد

## I Need to Acknowledge

The weight of certain news
on the phone
makes the receiver heavier

makes it fall from my hands

the pointless weight of certain things:
metal pieces in abandoned lots

the curved posture of my father
who after years
has yet to take my brother's corpse
off his shoulders
and place him in the ground

I need to acknowledge
to bear right along the road

After all, how many more minutes
can I continue walking
the middle of this freeway?

The blaring horns make me lonelier
and lonelier
and lonelier

Why do you bury the one who is left alone?

No death is natural
this poem won't make it to the hospital

## شعر بلندِ تنهایی

تکیه داده است به این وقتِ شب
و درجیرجیرِ سن‌وسالش جابه‌جا می‌شود
دمایش پایین آمده
که از چشم‌هاش برف می‌آید

بلند می‌شود، برود
پشتِ پنجره بنشیند
که می‌بیند ساعت‌هاست
پشتِ پنجره نشسته است

پرنده‌ای
به گوشه‌ی پوسیده‌ی آسمان نوک می‌زند . . .
آیا می‌خواهد زیباتر بمیرد؟
آیا برای مُردن همیشه باید بر زمین افتاد؟
آیا خاک،
دهانِ مُرده‌ها را پُر می‌کند
که آن‌چه را دیده‌اند، نگویند؟
آیا ریش‌هایش را بلند کرده است
که این‌همه پرسش را
در خطوطِ چهره‌اش پنهان کند؟

آیا می‌تواند بلند شود
زندگی‌اش را به منقار بگیرد
و تکه‌تکه آن را در دهانِ بچه‌هایش بگذارد؟

پنجره را باز می‌کند
پرتقال‌های حیاتِ خونی‌ست
دلیلِ ماه را نمی‌فهمد
دلیلِ آسمانِ این‌همه خالی را نمی‌فهمد
چراغ را خاموش می‌کند
و بر تختی که سال‌ها پیش
دور انداخته،
دراز می‌کشد.
او بَر دورها دراز می‌کشد

## Long Poem of Loneliness

He's leaning against this late hour
pushing open the creaking door of his age
his temperature drops
causing snow in his eyes.

He stands up
to go sit by the window
realizes he has been sitting
by the window for hours.

A bird
pecks at the corroded corner of the sky . . .
Does it want to die more beautifully?
Does one always need to fall to the ground in order to die?
Does the earth
fill the mouths of the dead
to stop them from describing what they've seen?
Has he grown his beard out
to conceal all these questions
in the creases of his face?

Is it possible to rise
to peck at bits of his life with his beak
and place them in his children's mouths?

He opens the window
the oranges of life are blood oranges
he does not understand the reason for the moon
he does not understand the reason for the all-empty sky.

He turns off the light
lies on the bed he discarded
years ago
he lies down upon the faraway

و بَر دورها به خواب می‌رود
و یک عمر راه را باید برگردد
وقتی که گوشی تلفن زنگ می‌زند

آن سوی خط
جنازه‌ی تکه‌تکه‌ی برادرش است
که با گوشیِ بی‌سیم در دستش منفجر شده
و حالا همان‌طور دارد آخرین جمله‌هایش را
از زمین جمع می‌کند

آن سوی خط زنی است
که از بیست و هفت سال پیش
تماس گرفته بگوید:
«عزیز من! شیرگاز، باز مانده
من مُرده‌ام
و حالا خواهرانت غم‌هایی هستند
که هر روز بزرگ‌تر می‌شوند . . .
از غم‌هایت مراقبت کن
به درس و مشق‌شان برس
با آن‌ها حرف بزن»

آن سوی خط منم
که می‌خواهم او را
از این شعر بیرون بیاورم
که می‌خواهم او را از این متن نجات دهم

اما
کسی نشسته است
بر سیم‌ها دست می‌کشد
اما کسی نشسته است
رابطه‌ام را با خودم شُنود می‌کند
و خِش‌خِشی که می‌شنوید
چاقویی‌ست که بر کلمات می‌کشد . . .
خون در سیم‌ها می‌چرخد

falls asleep upon the faraway
and when the phone rings,
he has to get back on a road as long as a man's life.

On the other side of the line
lies the severed corpse of his brother
who exploded while holding a phone in his hand
a corpse now gathering his last sentences
from the ground.

On the other end of the line
a woman
calls from twenty-seven years ago
just to say,
"Son, the oven gas is on
I am dead
and your sisters now
are sorrows growing taller every day . . .
Take care of your sorrows
attend to their homework
talk to them."

On the other end of the call
it is I
who want to haul him out of this poem
who want to save him from these words.

But someone is busy
scrutinizing the phone wires
someone is busy
a surveillance of my relationship with myself
and the scratchy noise you hear
is from his knife, carving out the words . . .
Blood circulates in the wires

و بوقِ ممتدِ قرمز
قطره
قطره
در گوشش فرو می‌ریزد

تنهاست
که گل‌های پیراهنش خشک می‌شوند
مردی
که چای در دهانش دم می‌کشد
مردی
که دکمه‌های زندگی‌اش باز مانده
و گوشه‌ای از روحش بیرون افتاده

نامه را
از کشو درمی‌آورد
خواندنَش بیش‌تر او را گرم خواهد کرد
یا سوزاندنَش؟

سیگارش را آتش می‌زند
و در میخِ کجی بر دیوار فرو می‌رود
دیروز گذشته است
فردا گذشته است
و دوردستِ خاکستریِ عمر
با هر پُکی به دهانش نزدیک‌تر می‌شود

او مرگ را از دو سمت لمس کرده است
مثلِ جلدِ همین کتاب
که نصفه می‌بندد
پرت می‌کند
بر زمین
نمی‌افتد
بلند می‌شود به هوا
و با دو خط از داستانش
بال می‌زند می‌رود

and the red eternity of the dial tone
pours into his ears
drop by drop.

It is his loneliness
that withers the flowers on his shirt.

The tea steeps in his mouth
his life's buttons have been left undone
and part of his soul is hanging out.

He draws the letter from the drawer
will he get warmer from reading it
or burning it?

He lights his cigarette
and drives it like a crooked peg into the wall
yesterday is over
tomorrow is over
and with each exhale the gray faraway of life
draws closer to his mouth.

He has touched both sides of death
like the front and back cover of this book
which he closes in the middle
tosses on the floor
but it doesn't fall
it rises
and flies off
with the two lines of its story.

حالا دارند چند پرنده‌ی سفید
چون کلماتی کوچک
از ذهن آسمان عبور می‌کنند

حالا دارند پرتقال‌ها را
به فصل‌های دیگری می‌برند

حالا دارند صحنه را
جمع می‌کنند

پلک‌هایش را پایین می‌کشد
و مثلِ لاک‌پشتی
در جهانِ سنگی‌اش ناپدید می‌شود

Now a couple of white birds
are crossing the sky's mind like tiny words.

Now they are carrying oranges
to other seasons.

Now they are leaving the stage
empty.

He draws shut the curtain of his eyelids
like a tortoise
retreating into its stony world.

## تردیدها و درنگ

به نام تو حتا
شک کرده‌ام
به درختان
و شاخه‌هایشان که شاید ریشه‌ها باشند
و شاید سال‌هاست که زیر زمین زندگی می‌کنیم

چه کسی جای جهان را عوض کرده است؟
و چرا پرندگان
در معده‌های ما پرواز می‌کنند؟
و چرا قرص‌ها تولدم را به تاخیر می‌اندازند؟
سال‌هاست
که زیر زمین زندگی می‌کنیم و
شاید
روزی از هفتاد سالگی‌ام به دنیا بیایم
و احساس کنم که مرگ
پیراهنی‌ست که به تن می‌کنیم
می‌توانی دکمه‌هایش را ببندی
یا باز بگذاری
می‌توانی آستین‌هایش را بالا بزنی
می‌توانی . . .

من
حدس‌های مردی زندانی‌ام
از فصل‌های پشت دیوار

## Doubts and a Hesitation

Even your name
I have doubts about
and about the trees
about their branches, if perhaps
they are roots
and we have been living
all these years underground.

Who has dislocated the world?
And why are birds circling in our stomachs?
Why does a pill defer my birth?
For years we've been living underground
and perhaps a day
in my seventies I'll be born
and feel that death
is a shirt we all come to put on,
whose buttons we can either fasten
or leave undone . . .
A man may roll up his sleeves
or he might . . .

I am the captive man's conjectures
about the seasons behind the wall.

## شعری برای صلح

با لوله‌ی تفنگ چای را هم می‌زند
با لوله‌ی تفنگ جدول را حل می‌کند
با لوله‌ی تفنگ فکرهایش را می‌خاراند

گاهی هم
روبه‌روی خودش می‌نشیند
و ترکش‌های خاطره را
از مغزش بیرون می‌کشد

در جنگ‌های زیادی جنگیده است
اما حریف تنهایی‌اش نمی‌شود

این قرص‌های سفید
کم‌رنگ‌ترش کرده‌اند
آن‌قدر که سایه‌اش بلند می‌شود
می‌رود، برایش آب می‌آورد

∎

باید قبول کنیم
که هرگز
هیچ سربازی
زنده از جنگ برنگشته است

## Poem for Stillness

He stirs his tea with a gun barrel
He solves the puzzle with a gun barrel
He scratches his thoughts with a gun barrel

And sometimes
he sits facing himself
and pulls bullet-memories
out of his brain

He's fought in many wars
but is no match for his own despair

These white pills
have left him so colorless
his shadow must stand up
to fetch him water

We ought to accept
that no soldier
has ever returned
from war
alive

## طرح ۲

رویم را بر می‌گردانم
و نیمی از جهان را از دست می‌دهم

## Pattern II

I turn my face away
and lose half the world.

# گردنبند

از ماه
لکه‌ای بر پنجره مانده است
از تمام آب‌های جهان
قطره‌ای برگونه‌ی تو

و مرزها آن‌قدر نقاشیِ خدا را خط‌خطی کردند
که خون خشک شده دیگر
نام یک رنگ است

از فیل‌ها
گردنبندی برگردن‌هایمان
و از نهنگ
شامی مفصل بر میز . . .

■

فردا صبح
انسان به کوچه می‌آید
و درختان از ترس
پشتِ گنجشک‌ها پنهان می‌شوند

## Necklace

Of the moon
all that's left is a stain upon the window.

Of all the waters in the world
this lone drop on your cheek.

And the borders have painted over God's landscapes for so long
that dried blood
is just a name for a color.

Tomorrow morning
humanity will enter the alley.
And the trees will hide
out of terror
behind the sparrows.

# فلاش‌بک

فرصتی نمانده است
بیا هم‌دیگر را بغل کنیم
فردا
یا من تو را می‌کشم
یا تو چاقو را درآب خواهی شست
همین چند سطر
دنیا به همین چند سطر رسیده است
به این که انسان
کوچک بماند بهتر است
به دنیا نیاید بهتر است

اصلا
این فیلم را به عقب برگردان
آن قدرکه پالتوِ پوستِ پشتِ ویترین
پلنگی شود
که می‌دود در دشت‌های دور
آن قدر که عصاها
پیاده به جنگل برگردند
و پرندگان
دوباره به زمین . . .
زمین . . . ؟

نه!
به عقب‌تر برگرد
بگذار خدا
دوباره دست‌هایش را بشوید
در آینه بنگرد
شاید
تصمیم دیگری گرفت

## Flashback

No time remains
Let's hold each other

Tomorrow
either I will murder you
or you will rinse the knife in water

These few lines
The world has come down
to these
few
lines

Is it better for a human to remain small
or not to be born?

            Or just
        rewind this movie
let the leather coat in the display window
become a leopard
leaping into distant fields
let every wooden walking cane
return to the forest on foot
And the birds
soar over the earth once more . . .
the earth . . .

       No!
            Rewind even further
Allow God
to wash his hands again
to gaze at the mirror
Perhaps
this time
he will come to a different decision

## طرح ۳

دریای بزرگ دور
یا گودال کوچك آب
فرقی نمی‌کند
زلال که باشی
آسمان در توست

## Pattern III

A large far sea
or a small puddle.
It makes no difference.

When you are translucent,
the sky appears in you.

# افتادن

نه خاک
نه دایره‌ای
در دفتر نقاشی دخترک
زمین
سری‌ست جدا شده از تن
چرخ می‌خورد میان هوا

ما چون فکرهای معلق می‌ریزیم
چون سطرهایی مبهم
بر دست‌های یک شاعر
و سکوتی طولانی
درگلوی سنگی قبرستان
می‌ریزیم
زرد بر پاییز و
سبز که هرچه می‌گردد
جایی برای نشستن پیدا نمی‌کند

می‌ریزیم
چون چای در فنجان ناصرالدین‌شاه و
قطره‌های خون در حمام فین

می‌ریزیم
ریز
ریز
ریز
چون برف
که هرگز هیچ‌کس ندانست
تکه‌های خودکشی یک ابر است

## Fall

Not soil
not a circle
in the child's sketchbook.

The Earth
is a severed head
rotating in midair.

We fall
like suspended thoughts
like vague lines
from a poet's hands
or like a lengthy silence
in the stony throat of a cemetery.

We fall
yellow upon the autumn.

What is still green
finds no place to thrive,
no matter how deep it roots.

We fall
like tea in Naser al-Din Shah's cup
like drops of blood in Fin Bathhouse.

We fall
minutely
like snowflakes
the ice slivers unknown to anyone
of a cloud's suicide.

می‌ریزیم
مثل بمب روی خاک
مثل خاک روی تو

می‌افتیم

این سیب هم برای تو دخترک!
دوباره فکرکن
نیوتن
هرگز آن چه را که باید
کشف نکرد

We fall
like bombs over the soil
like soil shoveled over us.

We fall.

This apple is yours, my child!
Think again!
Newton
could never find
what he intended to discover.

## لانگ اکسپوژر

آخرین پرنده را هم رها کرده‌ام
اما هنوز غمگینم

چیزی
در این قفسِ خالی هست
که آزاد نمی‌شود

## Long Exposure

Even after letting go
of the last bird
I hesitate

There is something
in this empty cage
that never gets released

## سوهان اضطراب

بعد تو آمدی
با تکه‌هایی از دیروقت، چسبیده به کفش‌هات.
شب را
از چوب‌رختی آویزان کردی
و در حمام پنهان شدی

حالا صدای سابیدنِ اتفاق می‌آید
صدای شستنِ چند ساعتِ گذشته
زیر شیرِ آب

عزیزِ من!
پنهان را نمی‌شود پنهان کرد
گلوله در گوشت حرف می‌زند
عزیزِ من!
گیرم که دستگیره‌ها را برق بیندازی
جای انگشتانت از روحِ آن‌ها پاک نخواهد شد

∎

صبح
از سفیدیِ دیوارها بیدار شدم
از سفیدیِ گلدان‌ها، پرده‌ها، پنجره‌ها
حتا در عکس‌ها هیچ‌کس پیدا نبود
دیروز، از پنج روزِ پیش پیدا نبود
وقتی ملافه را کنار زدم
پاهام پیدا نبود

تو
تا صبح همه‌چیز را سابیده بودی!

## Agony's Rasp

Then you arrived
with bits of late hours
stuck to your slippers.
You hung the night from the coat tree
and hid yourself in the bathroom.

Now the scraping off of incident,
the sound of washing the past few hours
into the sink.

My brother!
Humans cannot hide the hidden.
Not when bullets speak in the flesh.

Even if you polish all the doorknobs,
your fingerprints will not be wiped from their spirits.

In the morning
I woke to the polished walls,
the polished vases, curtains, windows.
No one was visible even in the pictures,
yesterday indistinct from five days ago.
When I pulled the sheet aside,
my feet were gone.

You
had scrubbed everything till morning.

## ادامه‌ی تصویر

دستت را دراز می‌کنی
اما
هرچه سر می‌کشم
ادامه‌ی تصویر پیدا نیست

چای را دم می‌کنیم؟
یا چمدان را می‌بندی؟

خوابی مبهم
درست مثل برگی در دست‌های باد
که نمی‌دانی
از زمین بَرش داشته
یا از درخت

## The Rest of the Picture

You extend your hand
yet no matter how much I strain to see
the rest of the picture remains unclear.
Will we brew tea?
Or will you pack your bags?

A blurred dream
like a leaf in the wind's invisible hands.
Unclear
whether the wind has lifted it
or released it from a tree.

## کدام پل

کدام پل
درکجای جهان
شکسته است
که هیچ‌کس به خانه‌اش نمی‌رسد

## What Bridge

What bridge
somewhere in the world
has collapsed
so that no one gets home?

## طرح ٤

خیره بر کره‌ی کوچک
دوباره حساب کرد
جایی برای جنگلِ بی‌انتها نبود
جایی برای دریایی که هرچه می‌روی
به پایانش نمی‌رسی

چشم‌های تو را آفرید.

## Pattern IV

Staring at the tiny planet
God calculated again.
There was no space for a continuous forest
no space for an infinite sea
no matter how endless the search.

And so the invention of your eyes.

## قایق کاغذی

یک جفت کفش
چند جفت جوراب با رنگ‌های نارنجی و بنفش
یک جفت گوشواره‌ی آبی
یک جفت ...
کشتی نوح است
این چمدان که تو می‌بندی!

بعد
صدای در
از پیراهنم گذشت
از سینه‌ام گذشت
از دیوارِ اتاقم گذشت
از محله‌های قدیمی گذشت
و کودکی‌ام را غمگین کرد

کودک بلند شد
و قایق کاغذی‌اش را بر آب انداخت
او جفت را نمی‌فهمید
تنها سوار شد،
آب‌ها به آینده می‌رفتند ...

همین جا دست بردم به شعر
و زمان را
مثل نخی نازک
بیرون کشیدم از آن!
دانه‌های تسبیح ریختند:


من       ...       تو
                  ...       کودکی

...               قایق کاغذی
نوح              ...
...               آینده
        ...

## Paper Boat

A pair of shoes
some pairs of socks in orange or purple,
a pair of blue earrings
a pair of . . .
This is Noah's ark
This luggage that you're packing!

Then the sound of the door
passed through my shirt
through my chest
through the wall of my room
through old neighborhoods
that distilled my school years.

The kid stood up,
launched his paper boat into the water.
He did not understand the sense of a "pair,"
so he boarded alone.
The waters moved toward the future . . .

I modified the poem here
and pulled time out
like a thin thread.

The beads fell off:

I      . . .      you
. . .                  childhood
paper boat          . . .
. . .                  Noah
. . .      future

         . . .

تو را
با کودکی‌ام
بر قایق کاغذی سوار کردم و
به دوردست فرستادم،
بعد با نوح
در انتظار طوفان قدم زدیم.

I brought you and my childhood
aboard the paper boat, left the dock.
Then I paced with Noah,
waiting for the storm.

## لانگ اکسپوژر ۲

مسافران سوار شدند
و ناخدا بادبان‌ها را کشید

دریا اما
صبح، زودتر بیدار شده بود
و پیش از آن‌ها
رفته بود

## Long Exposure II

The passengers board
and the pilots hoist the sails

but the sea
woke up even earlier,
departed
before all of them

## ملاقات

بارانی که روزها
بالای شهر ایستاده بود
عاقبت بارید،
تو بعدِ سال‌ها به خانه‌ام می‌آمدی

تکلیفِ رنگ موهات
در چشم‌هام روشن نبود
تکلیفِ مهربانی، اندوه، خشم
و چیزهای دیگری که در کمد آماده کرده بودم
تکلیفِ شمع‌های روی میز
روشن نبود . . .

من و تو بارها
زمان را
درکافه‌ها و خیابان‌ها فراموش کرده بودیم
و حالا زمان داشت
از ما انتقام می‌گرفت

در زدی
باز کردم،
سلام کردی
اما صدا نداشتی،
به آغوشم کشیدی
اما
سایه‌ات را دیدم
که دست‌هایش توی جیبش بود

به اتاق آمدیم
شمع‌ها را روشن کردم
ولی هیچ چیز روشن نشد
نور
تاریکی را
پنهان کرده بود . . .

## Meeting

The rain hovering over the city for days
finally fell.
You
were arriving after years . . .

I was in the dark
about your hair color
about passion, sorrow, fury
and about all else I had prepared in the drawers.
In the dark
about the candles on the table . . .

Repeatedly you and I
had forgotten about time in cafés and on the streets
and now time
is taking its revenge on us.

You knocked on the door,
I answered.
You greeted me
but had no voice,
gave me a hug
but I saw your shadow
with its hands kept in its pockets.
We stepped into a room,
lit the candles
but nothing in the room was lit.
The glow conceals the unlit . . .

■

بعد
بر مبل نشستی
در مبل فرو رفتی
در مبل لرزیدی
در مبل عرق کردی
پنهانی، گوشه‌ی تقویم نوشتم:

نهنگی که در ساحل تقلا می‌کند
برای دیدن هیچ کس نیامده است.

While you collapsed on the sofa
sank into it
shivered on it
sweated

I wrote,
surreptitiously,
on my calendar's margins:

A whale dying in agony on the beach
is not there to meet anyone.

# حدودِ صبح

مرتبش نمی‌کند
می‌گذارد صبح
همانطور چروک بماند
از دیشب

می‌ایستد روبه‌روی پنجره،
می‌گذارد مرگ
از دهانش پایین برود
بچرخد در سَرسَرای سینه‌اش
شیرِخون را باز بگذارد،
یادش برود . . .
می‌گذارد باد
بیاید
پیراهنِ افتاده بر صندلی را بپوشد،
برود . . .
می‌گذارد گلدان‌ها
یک بار هم که شده
هرطور دوست داشته باشند خشک شوند

می‌ایستد روبه‌روی آسمان
دست می‌کشد به موهایش،
می‌گوید:
پریدن، ربطی به بال ندارد
قلب می‌خواهد.

## Around Morning

She does not tuck the sheet of morning neatly,
leaves it wrinkled
from last night.

She stands at the window,
allows death
to slip down her throat
to circulate in the hall of her chest
to leave open the blood faucets
then to forget them all . . .

She allows the wind
to enter
to put on the shirt left on the chair,
then to exit.

She stands before the window,
strokes her hair, says:
Flying requires no wings,
only the heart, its chambers.

## طرح ٥

دزدی در تاریکی
به تابلوی نقاشی خیره مانده است

## Pattern V

In the dark
a burglar
stares at the painting

## تن دادن

و درد
که این‌بار پیش از زخم آمده بود
آن‌قدر درخانه ماند
که خواهرم شد.
با چرک پرده‌ها
با چروک پیشانی دیوار
کنارآمدیم
و تن دادیم
به تیک‌تاک عقربه‌هایی
که تکه‌تکه‌مان کردند.

پس زندگی همین قدر بود؟
انگشت اشاره‌ای به دوردست؟
برفی که سال‌ها
بیاید و ننشیند؟
و عمر
که هرشب از دری مخفی می‌آید
با چاقویی کُند

ماه
شاهد این تاریکی‌ست
و ماه
دهان زنی زیباست
که در چهارده شب
حرفش را کامل می‌کند
و ماهی سیاه کوچولو
که روزی از مویرگ‌های انگشتانم راه افتاده بود
حالا در شقیقه‌هایم می‌چرخد

## Acquiescence

And pain
which arrived this time prior to the wound
remained so long in our home
it became my sister.
We succumbed
to the dirt of the draperies,
to the furrows on the wall's forehead.
We succumbed
to the ticking hands of
the clock
as it dismembered us.

So was that all life could be?
An index finger pointing toward the faraway?
Snow falling for years
yet failing to take shape into piles?

And life
which enters from a hidden door every night
with a dull knife.

The moon is witness to
this darkness
and the moon is
the mouth of a lover
who consummates words
in fourteen nights

and the little black fish
moving through the capillaries of my fingers
is now orbiting my temples.

در من صدای تبر می‌آید!
آه، انارهای سیاه نخوردنی بر شاخه‌های کاج
وقتی که چارفصل به دورم می‌رقصیدند
رفتارتان چقدر شبیه‌ام بود.
در من
فریادهای درختی‌ست
خسته از میوه‌های تکراری.

من، ماهیِ خسته از آبم!
تن می‌دهم به تو
تور عروسی غمگین
تن می‌دهم
به علامت سوالِ بزرگی
که در دهانم گیرکرده است.
پس روزهایمان همین قدر بود؟!

و زندگی آن‌قدرکوچک شد
تا در چاله‌ای که بارها از آن پریده بودیم
افتادیم.

Within me
come the cries of a tree
tired of repeating the same fruit.

I am a fish tired of water!
I succumb to you,
sad birdcage veil
I succumb
to the giant question mark
stuck in my mouth.

So were our days only that long?

And life grew so narrow
that we fell
finally
into the same pit
we leapt over
many times
before.

## پرندهٔ اندوه

گلوله‌ای از گردنم عبور می‌کند
و خون در پَرهایم
به حرف در می‌آید

شکارچی نمی‌داند
شامی که می‌خورند
همه را غمگین خواهد کرد

شکارچی نمی‌داند
که بچه‌هایم همین حالا گرسنه‌اند
و من به طرزِ احمقانه‌ای
به پرواز ادامه خواهم‌داد

شکارچی نمی‌داند
که سال‌ها در درون‌شان بال بال خواهم زد
و کودکانش کم‌کم
به قفس بدل می‌شوند

## The Bird of Sorrow

A bullet passes through my neck
my blood
begins to speak through my feathers

The hunter doesn't know
the dinner his children are eating
will upset everyone

The hunter doesn't know
my children are hungry right now
and I will continue flying
in a foolish direction

The hunter doesn't know
I'll be flying in their stomachs for years
and his children
will turn slowly
into cages

## طرح ٦

پرواز هم
دیگر رویای آن پرنده نبود

دانه‌دانه پرهایش را چید
تا بر این بالِش
خواب دیگری ببیند.

## Pattern VI

Flying
was no longer the bird's wish

It plucked its feathers out
one by one,
in order to lie bald upon this pillow,
in order to slip into a different dream

## شخصیت‌ها

شخصیت‌هایی در من‌اند
که با هم حرف نمی‌زنند
که همدیگر را غمگین می‌کنند
که هرگز دورِ یک میز غذا نخورده‌اند

شخصیت‌هایی در من‌اند
که با دست‌هایم شعر می‌نویسند
با دست‌هایم اسکناس‌های مُرده را ورق می‌زنند
دست‌هایم را مُشت می‌کنند
دست‌هایم را بر لبه‌ی مبل می‌گذارند
و هم‌زمان
که این یکی می‌نشیند
دیگری بلند می‌شود، می‌رود

شخصیت‌هایی در من‌اند
که با برف‌ها آب می‌شوند
با رودها می‌روند
و سال‌ها بعد
در من می‌بارند

شخصیت‌هایی در من‌اند
که در گوشه‌ای نشسته‌اند
و مثلِ مرگ با هیچ‌کس حرف نمی‌زنند

شخصیت‌هایی در من‌اند
که دارند دیر می‌شوند
دارند پایین می‌روند
دارند غروب می‌کنند
و آن یکی هم نشسته است
روبه‌روی این غروب، چای می‌خورد

## Characters

There are characters in me
who do not talk to each other
who fill each other with grief
who have never dined at the same table

In me there are characters
who write their own poetry with my hands
who flip through stacks of bills with my hands
who make fists of my hands
who place my hands on the sofa edge
and while one sits down
the other stands up, leaves

In me there are characters
who melt in the snow
who drift with the rivers
and years later
rain into me

In me there are characters
who sit on a corner
and like death talk to no one

There are characters in me
who arrive too late
who are settling
and another one sitting
facing this sunset
sipping tea

شخصیت‌هایی در من‌اند
که همدیگر را زخمی می‌کنند
همدیگر را می‌کُشند
همدیگر را
در خرابه‌های روحم خاک می‌کنند

■

من اما
با تمام شخصیت‌هایم
دوستت دارم

In me there are characters
who stab each other
assassinate each other
bury each other
in the cemetery of my psyche

but I
with all of my characters
go on caring for you

## میزِ به هم ریخته

این میزِ به هم ریخته
جنازه‌ی یک مهمانی‌ست

من و تو که تنها بودیم
پس این‌همه ته سیگار بر کفِ اتاق‌ها
این چای‌های سرد
این کاغذهای مچاله
که در تصادف با عقل مُرده‌اند،
از کجا آمده است؟

■

تو
سال‌ها پیش رفته‌ای
و جسدهای من
در هر کجای این خانه
هر یک به کاری مشغول‌اند

## The Cluttered Table

This cluttered table
is the corpse of the party.

You and I were alone,
so where have all these
cigarette butts on the floor come from,
these cold cups of tea
these crumpled papers,
ruined in a collision with acuity?

You left years ago
and my inert bodies
are occupied with something
in every corner of this house.

# فدریکو گارسیا لورکا

کلماتت راکم قدم زدم
دانستم
چرا خونی که از قلب و
از پاهایم می‌گذرد
یکی است.

و چرا پنج عصر
گاهی تا ساعت‌ها بعد
در اتاقم می‌ماند.

من فکر می‌کنم
گلوله‌ای که سمت تو شلیک شد
لیوانی آب بود
بر جنگلی که آتش گرفته است.
و سوختن
در آتشی که تو بر پا کنی
لذتی‌ست
چون روشن کردنِ سیگار با خورشید

## Federico García Lorca

When I hiked in your words
I realized
why the blood passing through my heart
was the same as the blood
running through the veins of my legs.

And why five o'clock in the afternoon
would often remain in my room
long into the evening.

I think the bullet shot toward you
was a glass of water
poured on a forest in flames.

And burning in the blaze that you've lit
is a delight
like igniting a cigarette with the sun.

# لکه‌ای بر پیراهن یک سرباز

سوار شدیم و نمی‌دانستیم
این قطار
در ایستگاهی دیگر پیاده می‌شود
و دستی دیگر تفنگ‌های ما را پر کرده بود
دستی که تفنگ‌های آن‌ها را هم . . .

خاکِ نشسته بر این پوتین‌ها
مخلوطی‌ست از زنان و مردانی
که کودکانه ما را تقدیر نامیدند

خاک
خلاصه‌ی تمام حرف‌ها بود و
سرخ
مدادی قرمز
در دست‌های کودکی
که تازه اولین سیب‌های باغ را رنگ کرده است

■

نشانه گرفتیم، اما
جنگ
گلوله‌های رها شده در تاریکی‌ست
گاه دشمنت را می‌اندازی و
گاه دخترت را . . .

سوار شدیم و نمی دانستیم . . .
اصلاً
این بار دنیا را عوض می‌کنم
تفنگی را
که بر سینه‌ی این کودک گذاشته‌ام
به دست‌هایش می‌دهم تا بازی کند
با دشمنانم شام می‌خورم

## Stain on a Soldier's Uniform

We scrambled aboard,
unaware that the train
would stop at a different station,
not knowing another hand had loaded our guns,
hands that had loaded guns for them, too.

The dust on these boots
is a mixture of men and women
who, like children,
named this ending our fate.

The dust was the sum
of all that was said
and the red only a marker
in a child's hand
after blushing the garden's apples.

We aimed at our targets
but war
shed its bullets in the dark
now and then you shoot your enemy
now and then your daughter.

We scrambled aboard,
unaware.

But this time
I will transform the world—
the weapons on the child's lap
are only toys, make-believe.
I sit down to eat with my enemies.

سیگار و

عکسی به یادگار . . .

تا

در قابی از دیوارهای جهان بیاویزیم.

Take a cigar
then take a picture

to hang on
a wall within the universe.

## ایستگاه و سربازان

هنوز دست داشتم
که تو را بغل کنم
هنوز لب داشتم
که بگویم، ببوسمت
هنوز پا داشتم
و این سطرِ لعنتی
از سطرهای قبل دور شد
و از پله‌های تنهاييِ بزرگ بالا رفت

چیزی در رویاهامان می‌سوخت
و دود از قطار برمی‌خاست


■


حالا
من بازگشته‌ام مادر!

حالا
من، عذابِ توآم مادر!
من، جهنمِ توآم!

تو مجبوری
کهنه‌ی جهنمت را عوض کنی

و هیچ‌چیز غمگین‌تر از این نیست
که مجبور باشی
جهنمت را بغل کنی
جهنمت را ببوسی

## Station and Soldiers

I still had hands
to embrace you
still had lips
to ask you something more
still had legs
and this goddamn line of poetry
stepped back
and climbed the stairs of great despair

Something was incinerating in our dreams
and the steam kept rising from the train

■

Now,
I'm back, Mother!

Now,
I'm your torment, Mother!
I'm hell!

You have to change your hell's diapers

And nothing is more agonizing
than having
to embrace your hell
to kiss it

# مادونِ قرمز

می‌ترسانَدَم قطار،
وقتی که راه می‌افتد
و این‌همه آدم را
از آن‌همه جدا می‌کند

حالا نوبت باد است
بیاید،
چند دستمالِ خیسِ مچاله
و یک کلاهِ جامانده در ایستگاه را
بردارد، ببرد
بعد شب می‌آید
با کلاهی که باد برده بود،
آن را
بر ایستگاه می‌گذارد به شعبده،
ادامه‌ی شعر تاریک می‌شود . . .

از این‌جا
با دوربینِ مادونِ قرمز ببینید:
چند مرد، یک زن
که رفته بودند با قطار،
نرفته‌اند . . .
دستمالی را که باد برده بود
نبرده است
اصلاً ریل
کمی آن طرف‌تر تمام شده
و این قطارِ زنگ زده
انگار سال‌هاست
همان‌جا ایستاده‌است.
مسافرانش
حرف می‌زنند
قهوه می‌خورند
می‌خندند

## Infrared Camera

The train terrifies me
when it departs
and splits this many people
from that many.

Now it's the wind's turn
to arrive,
to heave and carry off
some damp, wrinkled handkerchiefs,
a top hat left behind at the station.

Then night slips in,
wearing the hat the wind's taken away.

The rest of the station grows dark . . .

From here on,
peer through the infrared camera:

Several men, a woman,
who departed on the train,
have not departed at all . . .

The handkerchief carried by the wind
hasn't been carried off.

A few meters away
the railroad ends
and this rusted train
seems to have stopped
for years.

Its passengers chat,
sip coffee,
laugh

و طوری به ساعت‌هایشان نگاه می‌کنند
که انگار نمی‌بینند
عقربه به استخوان‌شان رسیده است

keeping an eye on their wristwatches
as if deaf to how those clock hands
tick in their cells.

# دریا

می‌خواهم جنازه‌ام بر آب بیفتد
و ساعت‌ها
به ابرها خیره شوم

مُرده‌ام موج بردارد
قایقی باشم
که مسافرش را پیاده کرده است
و حالا بی‌خیالِ هر چیز
بر این ملافه‌ی آبی چُرت می‌زند

مرگ
می‌خواست این طور زیبا باشد
که ما خاکش کردیم

## Sea

I wish my corpse could float on water
and I could go on staring
for hours
at the wheeling seagulls

My vacant frame mirrors the waves
I could turn into a boat
come to drop off its passenger
and without a care in the world
fall asleep on the blue sheet of the sea

Death wanted to be this beautiful
but we buried it

## آواز مه

بلیت قطار را پاره می‌کنم
و با آخرین گله‌ی گوزن‌ها
به خانه برمی‌گردم

آن‌قدر شاعرم
که شاخه‌هایم شکوفه داده است!
و آوازم
چون مهی بر دریاچه می‌گذرد:
شلیک هر گلوله خشمی است
که از تفنگ کم می‌شود
سینه‌ام را آماده کرده‌ام
تا تو مهربان‌تر شوی.

## Fog Song

I rip up my train ticket
and with the last herd of deer
return home.

I am so much a poet
that my antlers have blossomed
and my song
passes across the lake like fog:
            Shooting each bullet is a rage
                        released with a shotgun.
I have prepared the trunk of my body
for the possibility of your kindness.

# برسیم‌های برق

و امروز
آن‌قدر شفافیم
که قاتلان درون‌مان پیداست

و دریای شهرمان
چنان خسته است
که عنکبوت
بر موج‌هایش تار می‌بندد

کاش
کسی این مارها را
عصا کند
و کاش آن‌که استخوان‌هایم را می‌جوید
شعرهایم را از بر نبود

■

زنبورها را مجبور کرده‌ایم
از گل‌های سمّی
عسل بیاورند.
و گنجشکی که سال‌ها
بر سیم برق نشسته
از شاخه‌ی درخت می‌ترسد

با من بگو
چگونه بخندم
وقتی که دور لب‌هایم را مین‌گذاری کرده‌اند

ما
کاشفان کوچه‌های بن‌بستیم
حرف‌های خسته‌ای داریم

این‌بار
پیامبری بفرست
که تنها گوش کند

## On Power Lines

So translucent are we today
that our inner murderers have turned obvious.

And the sea of our city is so sluggish
that spiders weave their cobwebs over its waves.

If only someone would turn these snakes into rods
If only the one who gnawed at my bones
did not know my poems by heart.

We have driven the bees
to make honey from poisonous flowers
And the sparrow that perched for years on the power lines
fears the branches of the trees.

Tell me how to manage my smile
when they have planted land mines all around my lips.

We are the discoverers of dead-end alleys
We have exhausted many a word
This time
send us a prophet who only listens.

# دیوانگی

پنهانت می‌کنم پشتِ پرده‌ها
زیر پوست
در کلمه
در دهان

پدیدار می‌شوی در ندیدارها . . .

دست بر دهانت می‌گذارم
و پنهانت می‌کنم در مرگ . . .
تابوت را می‌بندم
و تاریکیِ تو را
از تاریکیِ جهان جدا می‌کنم.

## Insanity

Behind the curtains I enshroud you
beneath the skin
under words
in mouths

You appear in the never-clear . . .

I rest my hand over your eyes
and conceal you in death . . .
Closing the casket
I separate your darkness
from the dark of the world

## لانگ اکسپوژر ۳

باد که می‌آید
خاکِ نشسته بر صندلی بلند می‌شود
می‌چرخد در اتاق
دراز می‌کشد کنار زن،
فکر می‌کند
به روزهایی که لب داشت

## Long Exposure III

Once the wind blows
the dust stirs on the chair
circulates in the room
lies down beside her

thinks of the days
when it had lips

# جنگل

چشم‌های بسته، بازترند
و پلک، پرده‌ای‌ست
که منظره را عمیق‌تر می‌کند

بُگذار
رودخانه از تو بُگذرد
و سنگ‌هاش در خستگی‌ات ته‌نشین شوند
بُگذار
بخشی زنده از مرگ باشی
و ریشه‌ها به اعماقت اعتماد کنند

جنگل،
تنها یک درخت است
که در هزاران شکل
از خاک گریخته است

# Forest

Closed eyes open wider
and the eyelid is a curtain
extending the landscape.

Let the river filter through you
let its sands deliver sediment into your heavy fatigue
let yourself be a living part of death
and let roots trust in your depth.

Forest,
you are a single tree
fleeing the earth
a thousand ways.

## پرندهی صلح

نه راهی به رویا میرسد
نه رویایی به راه

برمیگردم
به رنگهای رفتهی دنیا

به موهای مادرم
پیش از آنکه پدر ببافدش
به خاک
پیش از آنکه تو در آن به خواب روی
و آن کتاب کوچک غمگین
-پیامبر شدن در جزیرهی متروک-
از هم
به هم گریختهایم
از خاک
به زیر خاک
و انگار تمام جادهها را
با پرگار کشیده است
و انگار مرگ نقطهای است
که به پایان تمام جملهها میآید

و آن پرندهی کوچک
که رویای من و تو بود
در دهانش برگی گذاشتهاند
تا سکوت کند

از شب به شب گریختهایم

دستهایت را به تاریکی فرو بر
و هرچه را که لمس کردی
باور کن

## The Bird of Reconciliation

A road will not lead to a dream
nor a dream to a road.

I return
to the faded colors of the world

to my mother's hair
before my father braids it
to the soil
before you fall asleep in it
and to that small, poignant book
with its prophet on a deserted island—

From each other
we have fled toward each other
from the earth
into the earth.

And that little bird
that was my dream and yours

has a leaf forced into its mouth now
to keep it silent.

We have fled from night into night.

Dip your hands into that dark
and believe
whatever you touch.

## بلیت یک طرفه

پیله‌های بسیاری دیده‌ام
آویزان از درختی
در جنگل‌های دور
افتاده بر لبه‌ی پنجره
رها در جوب‌های خیابان.

هرچه فکر می‌کنم اما
یک پروانه بیش‌تر
در خاطرم نیست

مگر چند بار به دنیا آمده‌ایم
که این‌همه می‌میریم؟

چند اسکناس مچاله
چند نخ شکسته‌ی سیگار
آه، بلیت یک طرفه!
چیزی
غمگین‌تر از تو
در جیب‌های دنیا پیدا نکرده‌ام

-ببخشید، این بلیت . . . ؟

-پس گرفته نمی‌شود.

پس بادها رفته‌اند؟!
پس این درخت
به زرد ابد محکوم شد؟!
و قاصدک‌ها
آن‌قدر درکنج دیوار ماندند
که خبرهایشان از خاطر رفت؟!

## One-Way Ticket

Many a cocoon I've seen
hanging from a tree
                in distant forests
                on the window ledge
in the gutter.

Yet no matter how hard I think,
I can't recall
more than a single butterfly.

How many times are we born
that we die
so many times?

How many crumpled bills
How many crushed cigarettes

Oh, all the one-way tickets!
I haven't found anything
more sorrowful than you
in the pockets of the world.

—Excuse me, this ticket . . .

—It won't be taken back.

So are all the winds gone?
Has this tree
been condemned to an eternal yellow?
And did the dandelions wither so long
where the walls meet in the corner
that they've forgotten their news?

-بیهوده مشت به شیشه‌های این قطار می‌کوبی.
بیهوده صدایت را
به آن سوی پنجره پرتاب می‌کنی
ما
بازیگران یک فیلم صامتیم.

—You pound the windowpanes of this train to no avail.
In vain you hurl your voice to the other side of the window.
We
are the actors in a silent film.

# خرده‌های تاریکی

در سایه‌ی چیزی که نیست
نشسته است و
چیزی که نیست را ورق می‌زند

او تکه‌تکه بیدار می‌شود
و تکه‌تکه راه می‌افتد
و تکه‌های بسیارش، مرگ را کلافه کرده است

انگشتِ اشاره‌اش که از آسمان می‌گذرد
اجازه می‌گیرد
از او می‌پرسد:
غروب، جز برای غمگین کردن
به چه درد می‌خورد؟
-همین!
پرسشی که پاسخ است
تا ابد زنده می‌ماند
پس رهایش کن، بگذار برود!

■

دیوانه است او
که هر بار حرف می‌زند
دیوار به سمت دیگرش نگاه می‌کند

دیوانه است او
که همچنان به کندنِ شب ادامه می‌دهد
و خُرده‌های تاریکی را
زیر تخت پنهان می‌کند

دیوانه است او
که گفته بود می‌رود
اما رفت
و گفته بود می‌ماند
اما ماند
و گفته بود می‌خندد

## Bits of Darkness

In the shade of what is not
he sits
turning the pages of what is not.

He wakes sliver by sliver
and walks in slivers
And his many slivers
have afflicted death.

His index finger moves across the sky
asks for permission
asks him
What can a sunset cure
except sorrow?

That's all.
The question which is the answer
will remain long after us.
So leave it, let it go!

Insane is he
whose speech makes the walls
look in another direction.

Insane is he
who keeps excavating the night
to conceal the bits of darkness beneath his bed.

Insane is he
who said he would leave
but left

who said he would stay
but stayed

اما خندید.
دیوانه است او
که رفتن و ماندن و خندیدن را بی‌خیال شده
به کندنِ معنیِ «اما» فکر می‌کند.

دیوانه باید باشد
که با طناب
او را به سپیده‌دم بسته‌اند

دیوانه است او
که دیروز تیربارانش کرده‌اند و
هنوز به فرار فکر می‌کند

and who said he would laugh
but laughed . . .

Insane is he
who wouldn't leave or stay or laugh
and considers excavating the sense of "but."

He must be insane
this man tied by a rope to the sunrise.

He is insane
this man who was shot yesterday
who still plans his escape.

# لانگ اکسپوژر ٤

صدای قلب نیست
صدای پای توست
که شب‌ها در سینه‌ام می‌دوی

کافی‌ست کمی خسته شوی
کافی‌ست بایستی.

## Long Exposure IV

They aren't my heartbeats
They are your footsteps
running in my chest at night.

If you tire out it is enough.
Enough if you cease to run.

## عبور

وقتی کلید را
در جیب‌هایم پیدا نمی‌کنم
نگرانِ هیچ چیز نیستم

وقتی پلیس
دست بر سینه‌ام می‌گذارد
یا وقتی که پشتِ میله‌ها نشسته‌ام
نگرانِ هیچ چیز نیستم ...

مثلِ رودخانه‌ای خشک
که از سد عبور می‌کند
و هیچ‌کس نمی‌داند
می‌رود
یا بازمی‌گردد

## Passage

When I fail to find
the keys in my pockets
I'm not bothered.

When the police place their hands on my chest
or when I sit behind bars
I'm not bothered . . .

Just like
a riverbed
cutting through a dam
unclear
if it is leaving
or returning.

## لانگ اکسپوژر ۵

فراموش کن
مسلسل را
مرگ را
و به ماجرای زنبوری بیندیش
که در میانه‌ی میدان مین
به جستجوی شاخه گلی است.

## Long Exposure V

Forget about the machine gun
about death

and consider the saga of a bee
humming over minefields
in pursuit of a flower.

## مورچه

من مُرده‌ام
و این را فقط
من می‌دانم و تو
که چای را تنها در استکان خودت می‌ریزی

خسته‌تر از آنم که بنشینم
به خیابان می‌روم
با دوستانم دست می‌دهم
انگار هیچ اتفاقی نیفتاده‌است

-گیرم کلید را در قفل در بچرخانی
دلت باز نخواهد شد!

می‌دانم
من مُرده‌ام
و این را فقط من می‌دانم و تو
که دیگر روزنامه را با صدای بلند نمی‌خوانی

نمی‌خوانی و
این سکوت مرا دیوانه کرده است
آن‌قدر که گاهی دلم می‌خواهد
مورچه‌ای شوم
تا در گلوی نی‌لبکی خانه بسازم
و باد نُت‌ها را به خانه‌ام بیاورد
یا مرا از سیاهی سنگ‌فرش خیابان بردارد
بگذارد روی پیراهن سفید تو
که می‌دانم
باز هم مرا پرت می‌کنی
لابه‌لای همین سطرها
لابه‌لای همین روزها

## Ant

I am dead and
only you and I know this,
you who pour the tea into your cup alone.

Too tired to sit
I head to the streets,
shake my friends' hands
as though nothing has happened.

Even if you turned the key in the lock
your heart would not open.

I know
I am dead
and that
only you and I know,
you who no longer read the newspaper aloud.

You who no longer read at all
and the silence is so maddening
that I wish at times
to become an ant
to build a house in the throat of a flute
to ask the wind to blow the notes
to send them drifting into this window
or lift me out of the shadows on the flagstones,
to place me on your white shirt
where I know
you will shake me off again
within the lines of this poem
within these very days.

این روزها در خواب‌هایم تصویری‌ست

که مرا می‌ترساند

تصویری از ریسمانی آویخته از سقف

مردی آویخته از ریسمان

پشت به من

و این را فقط من می‌دانم و من

که می‌ترسم برش گردانم

In my dreams
these days contain an image
that scares me

an image of a rope hung from the ceiling
a man hanged by the rope
with his back to me
and only I know, I
who am terrified to turn him around.

## لانگ اکسپوژر ۶

به شانه‌ام زدی
که تنهایی‌ام را تکانده باشی

به چه دل خوش کرده‌ای؟!
تکاندن برف
از شانه‌های آدم‌برفی؟

## Long Exposure VI

You brushed my shoulder
to get off the loneliness.

What are you hoping for
brushing snow
from the shoulder of a snowman?

## نقطه‌ی سیاه

این سطر
یا سطرهای بعد
نقطه‌ای می‌آید
که پایان تمام حرف‌هاست

در قاب غمگین پنجره
موهای خسته و
پیراهن سیاه دخترکی که دور می‌شود
دور می‌شود
دور می‌شود

در قاب غمگین پنجره
نقطه‌ای سیاه
دور می‌شود
نقطه‌ای
که پایان تمام حرف‌هاست

# Dark Period

In this line
or the next one
there will be a period,
an end to all the words.

Within the stark frame of the window,
tired silhouettes
and the dark dress
of a little girl growing distant
                          growing distant
                                    growing distant

In the stark frame of the window
a dark period
grows distant.

A period
that is the end to all the words.

## لولای در

تیرِ هوایی بی‌خطر!
تو آسمان را گشتی

روز به سختی
از زیر در
از سوراخ کلیدها به درون آمد
اگر دست من بود
به خورشید مرخصی می‌دادم
به شب اضافه کار!
سیگاری روشن می‌کردم
و با دود
از هواکشِ کافه بیرون می‌رفتم . . .
مِه می‌شدم در خیابان‌ها
که لااقل
این‌همه گم شدن را
اتفاقی کنم

برادرم!
چگونه پیدایت کنم؟
وقتی به یاد نمی‌آورم
چگونه گُمَت کرده‌ام

چقدر کلمات تنهایند
چقدر تاریکی آمده‌است
چقدر کلمات در تاریکی جا عوض می‌کنند
چقدر طبیعت لاغر شده است

■

به چیزهایی در اتاق
که چیزهایی هم نیستند
خیره می‌شوم
و دل خوش می‌کنم
به جیرجیر پرنده‌ای
که در لولای در گرفتار است

## Door Hinge

Safe aerial gunfire!
You murdered the sky

The day labored in
from below the door
through the keyholes

If I were in charge
I would dismiss the sun
and pay the night overtime!

I'd light a cigarette
and slip out the café's vent
with the smoke . . .

I'd turn into the fog over the street
at least until
I could render accidental
these many losses

My brother!
How can I find you
when I don't remember
how I lost you?

How severe these words are
How the darkness seeps in
How often words switch places in the dark

I stare
at things in the room
that are not really things

and console myself
with the chirp of the bird
stuck in the door hinge

# آجرها

دروغ دیواری‌ست
که هر صبح آجرهایش را می‌چینی
بنّای بی‌حواس من!
در را فراموش کرده‌ای

آب تا گردنم بالا آمده
آجرها تا گردنم بالا آمده
آب تا لب‌هایم بالا آمده
آب بالا آمده . . .

من اما نمی‌میرم
من ماهی می‌شوم

## Bricks

Lies are a wall
whose bricks you lay every morning,
my distracted bricklayer,
you have forgotten about the door!

The water has risen to my neck
The bricks have risen to my neck
The water passing my lips now
The water rising and rising . . .

But I will not die
I will become a fish.

## گوشه‌ی دیوانه‌ی اتاق

عمقِ آخرین حرف‌ها
مثلِ ایستادن کنارِ دره‌ای
می‌ترساندم
و سنگ‌ریزه‌ای
که به اعماق
می‌غلتد
همه‌چیز را با خود بُرده است

ماجرا برای تو کوچک بود
مثلِ سوزنی که در قرنیه‌ام فرو کنی
و تازه می‌فهمم
این رگِ سرخِ کاموا
که روزهاست بر میز رها شده،
از گردنم شکافته است

نبودنت نقشه‌ی خانه را عوض کرده
و هرچه می‌گردم
آن گوشه‌ی دیوانه‌ی اتاق را
پیدا نمی‌کنم

احساس می‌کنم
کسی که نیست
کسی که هست را
از پا در می‌آورد

## The Mad Corner of the Room

The depth of final words
frightens me
like standing at the rim of a valley

And the tiny stone
                    spiraling
                        down
                                into the deep
has taken everything with it

You saw the story, small
as a needle you could drive into my cornea

And only now do I realize
how the red vein of yarn
left for days on the table
has unraveled from my neck.
Your absence
has altered the map of this house
and no matter how much I search
I can't find
that mad corner of the room

I can feel
how the person who isn't
overwhelms
the person who is

**طرح ۷**

زیر این آسمان ابری
به معنای نامش فکر می‌کند
گل آفتابگردان

## Pattern VII

Under the overcast sky
the sunflower
thinks about the sense of its name

## شعری زخمی بر میز

حتا صبح
غروب کرده است

شعری زخمی بر میز
آخرین سطرهایش را بغل گرفته
نگاهم می‌کند

باد می‌آید
به موهایم دست هم نمی‌زند
شعله‌ای را در اعماقم
خاموش می‌کند
می‌رود

می‌دانم این مجسمه هم اگر پا داشت
مرا ترک کرده بود

تنهایی
زخمی‌ست که از تن بزرگ‌تر است
و این در
حتا اگر به جهنم باز شود
خوشحالم می‌کند

## Injured Poem on the Table

Even the new dawn has set

Staring at me from the table
an injured poem
has accepted its last lines

The wind blows
without brushing a single strand
of my hair
It blows out a flame within me
and departs

If this statue had legs
I know
it would leave me as well

Seclusion
is a wound larger than the body
and this door
even if it opens onto hell
will bring me joy

# بازی

بازی را عوض می‌کنی
و خود را از طنابی می‌آویزی
که سال‌ها پیش بر آن تاب خورده‌ای

ما
تکرار تکه‌های همیم

مثل تو پسرم که تاب می‌خوری
مثل من
که تو را تاب می‌دهم
تا طناب را فراموش کنم

# Game

You change the game
and hang yourself from the rope
you swung on
years ago.

We are the repetitions
of the pieces
of each other

like you, my son, on this swing
as I who swing you
to forget the rope.

## ابهام قفل‌ها

نه خورشید به سیاهی عادت می‌کند
نه من
به تاریکی فال این فنجان
نه خورشید به سیاهی عادت می‌کند
نه من
به رنگ‌های رفته‌ی این اتاق
درها و قفل‌های بسته مرا زنده می‌کند
این که فردا می‌آیی
نه آن که دیروز آمده‌ای

این که نیستی
نه آن بوسه‌های بنفش

درها و قفل‌های بسته مرا زنده می‌کند
جنگلی در مه
نه درختان ظهر تابستان

ابهام مرگ
نه یک تولد روشن

درها و قفل‌های بسته تو را . . .
شعری که خوانده‌ای نه
سطرهای مانده تو را زنده می‌کند
گوش کن:

## Sealed Doors

The sun won't conform to the dark
nor will I
to the black fortune of this cup.

The sun won't conform to the dark
nor will I
to the bleached walls of this room.

What revives me
is the sealed door

tomorrow's return
not yesterday's arrival
your absence
not this embrace

What revives me
are the sealed doors

Fog over the forest
not trees on a warm afternoon
death's opacity
not birth's luminosity

For you, the sealed rooms,
the remaining lines—
not the poem you've already read—
may revive you.
Just listen:

## لانگ اکسپوژر ۷

موسیقیِ عجیبی‌ست مرگ
بلند می‌شوی
و چنان آرام و نرم می‌رقصی
که دیگر هیچ‌کس
تو را نمی‌بیند

## Long Exposure VII

It is a strange music
death

You stand up
and dance so smoothly and softly
that nobody can see you
any longer

# Acknowledgments

Sincerest thanks to the following journals and outlets in which several of these poems have appeared or are forthcoming, some in slightly different form:

*The Arkansas International*: "Border," "Pattern," "Poem for Stillness," and "On Power Lines"

*The New Republic*: "I Need to Acknowledge" (originally "We Need to Acknowledge")

*Adroit Journal*: "Long Poem of Loneliness," "Meeting," and "One-Way Ticket"

*Guernica*: "Doubts and a Hesitation"

*The Literary Review*: "Necklace"

*Two Lines*: "Long Exposure," "The Cluttered Table," "Fog Song," and "Long Exposure VII"

*Poetry Daily*: "Acquiescence" and "The Bird of Sorrow"

*Jewish Currents*: "The Bird of Sorrow"

*The Slowdown*: "Characters"

*Circumference*: "Infrared Camera" and "Sealed Doors"

*The New York Times Magazine*: "Dark Period"

# About the Author

**Garous Abdolmalekian**, born in 1980, is an acclaimed Iranian poet and the author of seven books of poetry: *The Hidden Bird* (2002), *The Faded Colors of the World* (2005), *Lines Change Places in the Dark* (2008), *Hollows* (2011), *Nothing Is as Fresh as Death* (2012), *Acceptance* (2015), and *The Middle East Trilogy: War, Love, Loneliness* (2019). He is the recipient of the Karnameh Poetry Book of the Year Award (2003) and the Iranian Youth Poetry Book Prize (2006). His poems have been translated into French, German, Arabic, Swedish, Kurdish, Turkish, Polish, Russian, and Spanish. Abdolmalekian is currently the editor of the poetry section at Cheshmeh Publications in Tehran.

© 2014 Kari Jantzen

# About the Translators

**Ahmad Nadalizadeh** is a doctoral candidate in comparative literature at the University of Oregon. He is currently completing his dissertation, which examines the role of repetition in the aesthetic remediation of monumental traumas in twentieth-century Iran.

**Idra Novey** is the author of *Those Who Knew*, a finalist for the 2019 Clark Fiction Prize that was named a Best Book of the Year by over a dozen media outlets, including NPR, *Esquire*, BBC, *O, The Oprah Magazine*, and *Kirkus Reviews*. Her first novel, *Ways to Disappear*, won the 2016 Sami Rohr Prize and a Brooklyn Public Library prize, and was a finalist for the Los Angeles Times Book Prize for First Fiction. Her most recent poetry collection, *Exit, Civilian*, was selected for the 2011 National Poetry Series by Patricia Smith. For her poetry and translations, Novey has received awards from the National Endowment for the Arts, the PEN Translation Fund, and the Poetry Foundation. She teaches in the creative writing program at Princeton University.

GAROUS ABDOLMALEKIAN
*Lean Against This Late Hour*

PAIGE ACKERSON-KIELY
*Dolefully, a Rampart Stands*

JOHN ASHBERY
*Selected Poems*
*Self-Portrait in a Convex Mirror*

PAUL BEATTY
*Joker, Joker, Deuce*

JOSHUA BENNETT
*The Sobbing School*

TED BERRIGAN
*The Sonnets*

LAUREN BERRY
*The Lifting Dress*

JOE BONOMO
*Installations*

PHILIP BOOTH
*Lifelines: Selected Poems 1950–1999*
*Selves*

JIM CARROLL
*Fear of Dreaming: The Selected Poems*
*Living at the Movies*
*Void of Course*

ALISON HAWTHORNE DEMING
*Genius Loci*
*Rope*
*Stairway to Heaven*

CARL DENNIS
*Another Reason*
*Callings*
*New and Selected Poems 1974–2004*
*Night School*
*Practical Gods*
*Ranking the Wishes*
*Unknown Friends*

DIANE DI PRIMA
*Loba*

STUART DISCHELL
*Backwards Days*
*Dig Safe*

STEPHEN DOBYNS
*Velocities: New and Selected Poems 1966–1992*

EDWARD DORN
*Way More West*

ROGER FANNING
*The Middle Ages*

ADAM FOULDS
*The Broken Word: An Epic Poem of the British Empire in Kenya, and the Mau Mau Uprising Against It*

CARRIE FOUNTAIN
*Burn Lake*
*Instant Winner*

AMY GERSTLER
*Dearest Creature*
*Ghost Girl*
*Medicine*
*Nerve Storm*
*Scattered at Sea*

EUGENE GLORIA
*Drivers at the Short-Time Motel*
*Hoodlum Birds*
*My Favorite Warlord*
*Sightseer in This Killing City*

DEBORA GREGER
*By Herself*
*Desert Fathers, Uranium Daughters*
*God*
*In Darwin's Room*
*Men, Women, and Ghosts*
*Western Art*

TERRANCE HAYES
*American Sonnets for My Past and Future Assassin*
*Hip Logic*
*How to Be Drawn*
*Lighthead*
*Wind in a Box*

NATHAN HOKS
*The Narrow Circle*

ROBERT HUNTER
*Sentinel and Other Poems*

MARY KARR
*Viper Rum*

WILLIAM KECKLER
*Sanskrit of the Body*

JACK KEROUAC
*Book of Blues*
*Book of Haikus*
*Book of Sketches*

JOANNA KLINK
*Circadian*
*Excerpts from a Secret Prophecy*
*Raptus*

JOANNE KYGER
*As Ever: Selected Poems*

ANN LAUTERBACH
*Hum*
*If in Time: Selected Poems 1975–2000*
*On a Stair*
*Or to Begin Again*
*Spell*
*Under the Sign*

CORINNE LEE
*Plenty*
*Pyx*

PHILLIS LEVIN
*May Day*
*Mercury*
*Mr. Memory & Other Poems*

PATRICIA LOCKWOOD
*Motherland Fatherland Homelandsexuals*

WILLIAM LOGAN
*Macbeth in Venice*
*Madame X*
*Rift of Light*
*Strange Flesh*
*The Whispering Gallery*

J. MICHAEL MARTINEZ
*Museum of the Americas*

ADRIAN MATEJKA
*The Big Smoke*
*Map to the Stars*
*Mixology*

MICHAEL McCLURE
*Huge Dreams: San Francisco
and Beat Poems*

ROSE McLARNEY
*Forage*
*Its Day Being Gone*

DAVID MELTZER
*David's Copy:
The Selected Poems of
David Meltzer*

ROBERT MORGAN
*Dark Energy*
*Terroir*

CAROL MUSKE-DUKES
*Blue Rose*
*An Octave Above Thunder:
New and Selected Poems*
*Red Trousseau*
*Twin Cities*

ALICE NOTLEY
*Certain Magical Acts*
*Culture of One*
*The Descent of Alette*
*Disobedience*
*For the Ride*
*In the Pines*
*Mysteries of Small Houses*

WILLIE PERDOMO
*The Crazy Bunch*
*The Essential Hits of
Shorty Bon Bon*

DANIEL POPPICK
*Fear of Description*

LIA PURPURA
*It Shouldn't Have Been
Beautiful*

LAWRENCE RAAB
*The History of Forgetting*
*Visible Signs: New and
Selected Poems*

BARBARA RAS
*The Last Skin*
*One Hidden Stuff*

MICHAEL ROBBINS
*Alien vs. Predator*
*The Second Sex*

PATTIANN ROGERS
*Generations*
*Holy Heathen Rhapsody*
*Quickening Fields*
*Wayfare*

SAM SAX
*Madness*

ROBYN SCHIFF
*A Woman of Property*

WILLIAM STOBB
*Absentia*
*Nervous Systems*

TRYFON TOLIDES
*An Almost Pure Empty
Walking*

SARAH VAP
*Viability*

ANNE WALDMAN
*Gossamurmur*
*Kill or Cure*
*Manatee/Humanity*
*Trickster Feminism*

JAMES WELCH
*Riding the Earthboy 40*

PHILIP WHALEN
*Overtime: Selected Poems*

ROBERT WRIGLEY
*Anatomy of Melancholy and
Other Poems*
*Beautiful Country*
*Box*
*Earthly Meditations:
New and Selected Poems*
*Lives of the Animals*
*Reign of Snakes*

MARK YAKICH
*The Importance of Peeling
Potatoes in Ukraine*
*Spiritual Exercises*
*Unrelated Individuals
Forming a Group Waiting
to Cross*